Brimming with creative inspiration, how-to projects, and useful information to enrich your everyday life, Quarto Knows is a favorite destination for those pursuing their interests and passions. Visit our site and dig deeper with our books into your area of interest: Quarto Creates, Quarto Cooks, Quarto Homes, Quarto Lives, Quarto Drives, Quarto Explores, Quarto Gifts, or Quarto Kids.

First published in Spanish as *El jardín mágico*
© 2016 Lemniscates
© 2016 Ediciones Ekaré. Barcelona. Spain

Published in English in 2018 by Walter Foster Jr.,
an imprint of The Quarto Group.
6 Orchard Road, Suite 100, Lake Forest, CA 92630, USA.
T (949) 380-7510 F (949) 380-7575 **www.QuartoKnows.com**

Walter Foster Jr. titles are also available at discount for retail, wholesale, promotional, and bulk purchase. For details, contact the Special Sales Manager by email at specialsales@quarto.com or by mail at The Quarto Group, Attn: Special Sales Manager, 401 Second Avenue North, Suite 310, Minneapolis, MN 55401 USA.

ISBN: 978-1-63322-513-8

Printed in China
10 9 8 7 6 5 4 3 2 1

FSC
www.fsc.org
MIX
Paper from responsible sources
FSC® C101537

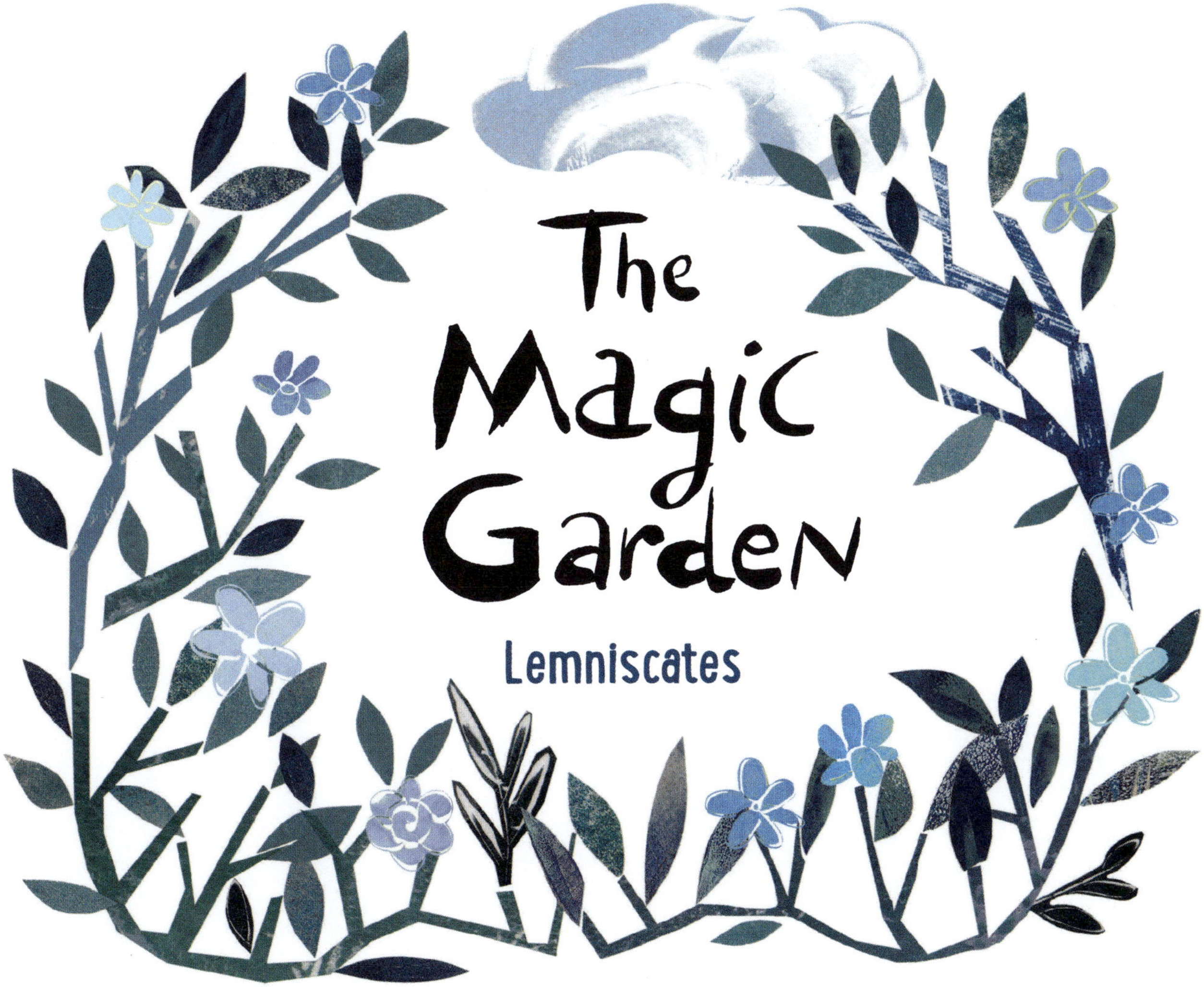

# The Magic Garden

### Lemniscates

Chloe lives in a magic garden,
but she doesn't even know it.

One autumn afternoon, Chloe walks by a colorful tree.
The branches sway softly in the breeze,
trying to get her to notice them.
But Chloe doesn't even see the tree.

Suddenly, Chloe hears something.
She leans in closer to the tree.
The wind seems to whisper to her:

Look at these colorful leaves! Soon, winter will come
and these leaves will fall to the ground.
But in the spring, new leaves will come!

Have you ever really looked at this garden?

Wonderful, amazing changes happen here every day. Sleepy caterpillars transform into beautiful butterflies that fly off to explore the world.

At night in this garden, there are insects that shine as bright as stars in the dark sky. Others gather in choirs to sing to the moon.

Many shy creatures live in this garden too. Some borrow the colors of their surroundings to hide themselves.

They dare to ask, "Can you find me?"

Others in this garden are known for their bad tempers.
They show off their bright colors to warn everyone,
saying, "Don't get too close!"

There are snakes in this garden
that can perform incredible feats,
like eating a meal three times their size.

In this garden,
birds weave wonderful nests
and spiders spin spectacular webs.

The bees in this magical garden
dance delicately through the breeze,
telling of where to find the best flowers.

When springtime arrives,
the trees are filled with beautiful blossoms.
The bees take nectar from the flowers
and turn it into sweet honey.

From the same flowers, fruits are born.
And from those fruits, new seeds.
And if a seed drops to the ground,
It soon grows into a new tree.
And the magic starts all over again.

The wind has told Chloe many
secrets of this magical garden.
Now it softly sways and whispers again:

"Magic... magic... magic..."

to remind her that there is magic all around
to explore and discover.

## How do caterpillars transform into butterflies?

The caterpillar is actually a baby butterfly, and it has to make a big change in order to become an adult. It must go from crawling on the ground to flying in the sky and from chewing its food to sucking it from flowers. People change very slowly over many years to grow up, but caterpillars must change very quickly to become butterflies. They lock themselves in cocoons made of silk called *chrysalises*. There they stay quiet and don't eat until the transformation is complete. When ready, the cocoon opens and the butterfly flies out. Later that butterfly will lay eggs and new caterpillars will be born, starting the cycle again.

## Why do fireflies glow?

On summer nights, with a little luck, we might discover fireflies in a tree or under some leaves. These insects generate light to find partners. Males have wings and fly through the night sending light signals to the females. Females don't have wings and stay where they can be seen, curving their bodies so the small light in their tail shows, like very tiny lanterns. Scientists don't know exactly how they turn their lights on and off or how fireflies can produce such bright light without creating much heat. It's magical!

## Why do animals camouflage themselves?

Some animals can blend in with their surroundings so they don't get noticed. That's what *camouflage* means. Camouflage can protect an animal from being seen, but it can also be useful for hunting. Insects are masters of camouflage and may take on the appearance of small branches, leaves, or flowers, adopting their colors. There are also other types of camouflage, for example, with sound. Moths make ultrasounds that confuse their predators' radars. Reptiles are also camouflage experts. Chameleons change the color of their skin according to what is around them. Some birds use camouflage too. Owl feathers look so much like the bark of a tree that they're almost invisible. The same goes for many fish that look just like the rocks and coral where they live, making it hard to see them unless they move.

## Why do animals have bright colors?

Just like camouflage, bright colors often protect an animal. But instead of hiding, some animals have bright colors to stand out from their surroundings and let their enemies know they're dangerous. It's as if they're saying: "Don't get too close, I might hurt you!" or "Don't try to eat me! You'll get poisoned!" Usually, bright colors mean that the animal is poisonous. For example, poison dart frogs, some salamanders, and the coral snake all have bright colors. The most common colors in nature to warn about danger are black and yellow.

## How can snakes eat meals that are bigger than they are?

Snakes' jaws are very flexible and allow their mouths to stretch like an open bag. A snake is able to catch prey up to three times bigger than its head. Without a sternum to connect their ribs, the food can go easily through them. Snakes don't chew; they swallow their prey whole. They use their sharp teeth to keep their prey from getting away. After swallowing a large meal, snakes remain still for days or weeks until they have digested all of the food.

## How and why do spiders and birds spin and weave?

Spiderwebs are made with liquid silk that spiders keep in their bellies. When they throw it out, the liquid becomes a solid thread of silk, ready to weave.  Some spiders are capable of producing threads of different thicknesses, and some are even stronger than a proportionate thread of steel! The key to building a spiderweb is in the wind. When spinning a web, the spider moves with the wind to give the thread shape and direction. First, she throws a strong thread that works as a bridge. She uses the bridge as a starting point for more threads to create a web. Whatever pattern the spider uses, the point of the web is to catch bugs, so the spider has its meal trapped and ready to eat.

Birds weave to build their nests. When it's time to lay their eggs, they need a safe environment where their chicks can be born. Just like spiders, they learn by instinct. Instinct tells them what size the nest should be and even how many eggs they might lay. Most birds search for small branches, blades of grass, leaves, or feathers to build their nests. They use thicker branches to build the main structure. Then they weave smaller and thinner branches and leaves and feathers to make the inside soft and comfortable, like a snuggly blanket.

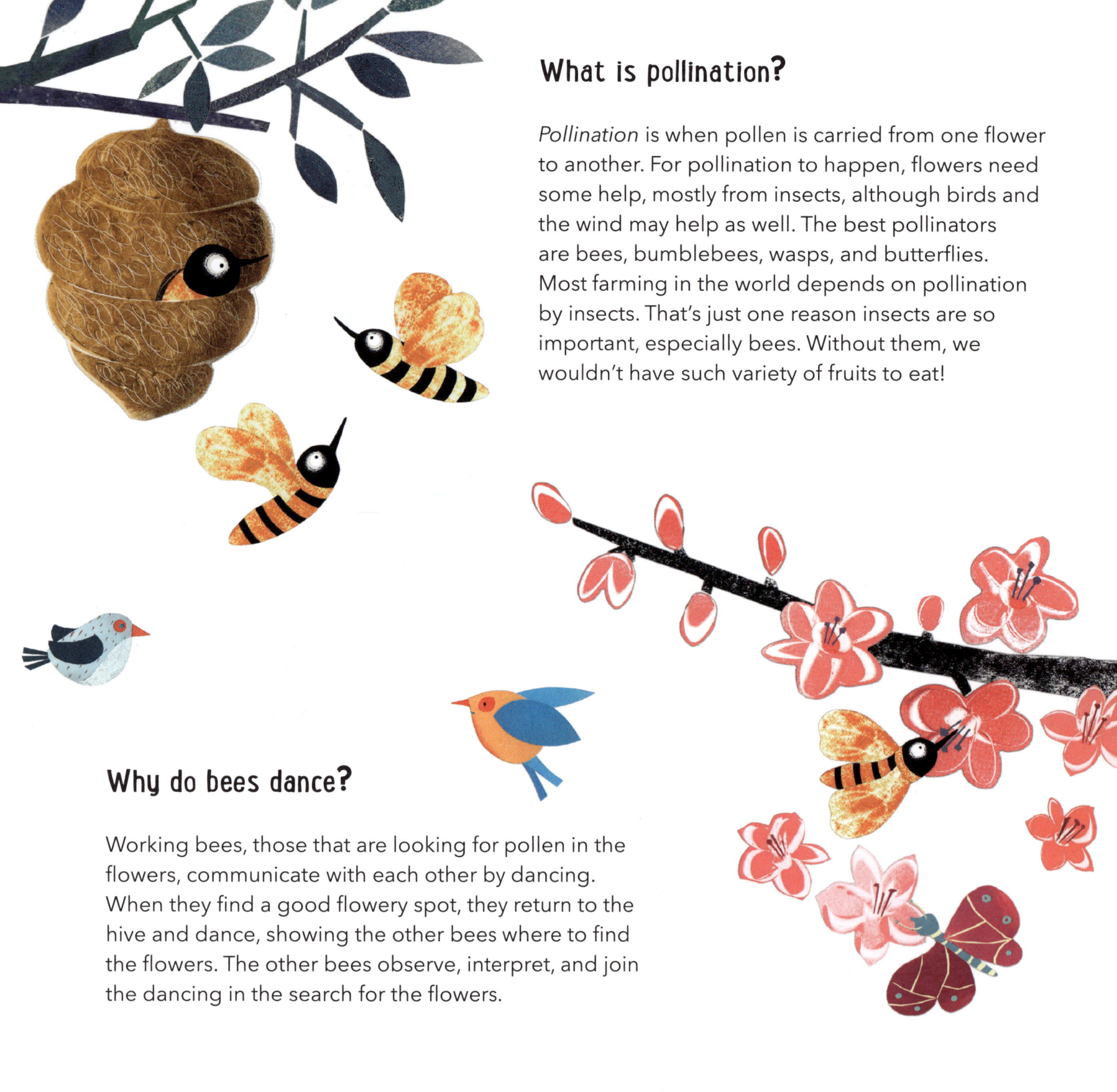

## What is pollination?

*Pollination* is when pollen is carried from one flower to another. For pollination to happen, flowers need some help, mostly from insects, although birds and the wind may help as well. The best pollinators are bees, bumblebees, wasps, and butterflies. Most farming in the world depends on pollination by insects. That's just one reason insects are so important, especially bees. Without them, we wouldn't have such variety of fruits to eat!

## Why do bees dance?

Working bees, those that are looking for pollen in the flowers, communicate with each other by dancing. When they find a good flowery spot, they return to the hive and dance, showing the other bees where to find the flowers. The other bees observe, interpret, and join the dancing in the search for the flowers.

This is the magic
that Chloe found in her garden...
just a tiny bit of all the magic
you can discover in nature!